Grade
4

PROBLEM SOLVING

Written by **Christine Hood**

Illustrated by **Dave Garbot**

FlashKids

This book belongs to

_____

Flash Kids
A Division of Barnes & Noble
122 Fifth Avenue
New York, NY 10011

ISBN: 978-1-4114-9925-6

Please submit all inquiries to FlashKids@bn.com

Printed and bound in China

Dear Parent,

Learning to solve problems is one of the most important skills in math. *Problem Solving* will help your child to look at problems with a critical eye. This book includes fun activities that help your child use logic, estimate, and choose a method to solve a problem. To get the most from *Problem Solving*, follow these simple steps:

- Provide a comfortable and quiet place for your child to work.
- Encourage your child to work at his or her own pace.
- Help your child with the problems if he or she needs it.
- Offer lots of praise and support.
- Encourage your child to work independently to gain confidence in his or her problem solving skills.
- Allow your child to enjoy the fun actvities in this book.
- Most of all, remember that learning should be fun!

Visit us at *www.flashkidsbooks.com* for free downloads, informative articles, and valuable parent resources!

School Carnival

Read each problem carefully and then solve it. Show your work.

1. Jake is working at the popcorn stand. He started the day with 22 bags of popcorn. At noon he had 11 bags left. How many bags did Jake sell?
   Name the operation you will use to solve the problem: __22 – 11=__
   Answer: _____11_____

2. Staci works in the goldfish game booth. She usually gives away 5 goldfish per hour. She's been working for 4 hours. How many goldfish has she given away?
   Name the operation you will use to solve the problem: _____
   Answer: _____

3. Mrs. Lopez made 64 cupcakes for the dessert booth. She sold all the cupcakes by noon. The children bought 2 cupcakes each. How many children bought cupcakes?
   Name the operation you will use to solve the problem: __64 ÷ 2=__
   Answer: ___32_____

4. Amir is selling hot dogs at 25¢ each. If 8 children bought hot dogs, how much money has Amir made?
   Name the operation you will use to solve the problem: _____
   Answer: _____

Number Game

Manuel works in the Numbers Game booth.

If players get six problems right, they win a prize.

Read the clues and see if you can solve the problems.

Clues:

1. Each problem has one step.

2. Use one operation sign (x, −, +, ÷).

3. Use one equals sign (=).

4. Some problems can have more than one answer.

Examples: 42 _____ 7 _____ 6   12 _____ 14 _____ 26

Answers: 42 ÷ 7 = 6   12 + 14 = 26

                  OR   42 = 7 x 6

1.
24 __✗__ 2 __=__ 48

2.
18 __−__ 50 __=__ 32

3.
15 __+__ 25 __=__ 40

4.
56 __=__ 7 __✗__ 8

5.
85 __−__ 62 __=__ 23

6.
9 __✗__ 8 __=__ 72

More Number Games

These problems are even harder.

Read the clues and see if you can solve the problems.

Clues:

1. Each problem has two steps.

2. Use two operation signs (x, −, +, ÷).

3. Use one equals sign (=).

Example: 1 _____ 4 _____ 2 _____ 3

Answer: (1 + 4) − 2 = 3

1.
(4 _____ 6) _____ 9 _____ 15

2.
(55 _____ 11) _____ 5 _____ 25

3.
38 _____ (6 _____ 6) _____ 2

4.
28 _____ (4 _____ 7) _____ 56

5.
(8 _____ 7) _____ 43 _____ 13

6.
72 _____ (81 _____ 9) _____ 8

Taking Steps

Some problems have more than one step.
Carefully read each problem. Then decide which steps
you should take to solve it. Write the steps in order.

Example: The Ferris wheel costs 5¢. Lin has 2 quarters and 2 dimes.
How many times can she ride the Ferris wheel?

Step 1: Find out how much money Lin has:

 = 70¢

Step 2: Divide 70¢ by the cost of one Ferris wheel ride: 70 ÷ 5 = 14
Answer: Lin can ride the Ferris wheel 14 times.

1. Hector won 6 bags of marbles. Each bag has 10 marbles.
   If Hector gives 3 friends an equal number of marbles,
   how many marbles would he give each friend?
   Step 1: _____
   Step 2: _____
   Answer: _____

2. Jenni had $\frac{9}{10}$ of a bag of popcorn. She ate $\frac{3}{10}$ of the bag.
   Then her sister ate $\frac{2}{10}$ of the bag. How much popcorn is left?
   Step 1: _____
   Step 2: _____
   Answer: _____

3. Brett started with 32 baseball cards. He sold 8 cards. Then he
   bought 12 more. How many cards does he have now?
   Step 1: __32 - 8 = 24_____
   Step 2: __24 + 12 =_____
   Answer: _____36_____

Pick Your Pizza

You can pick any two toppings you want at Peppy's Pizza booth.
All pizzas come with cheese. The topping choices are: pepperoni,
mushrooms, ham, olives, and peppers.

List the possible topping combinations.

Possible Combinations:

_____	and	_____	
Pepperoni	and	Peppers	
Mushrooms	and	Olives	
ham	and	Peppers	
_____	and	_____	
_____	and	_____	
_____	and	_____	
_____	and	_____	
_____	and	_____	
_____	and	_____	

Cookie Creations

In the Cookie Creations booth, children can decorate their own cookies!
Look at the chart, then answer the questions.

Sugar Cookie Recipe

Ingredient	2 dozen	6 dozen	12 dozen
shortening	1 cup		
sugar	$1\frac{1}{2}$ cups		
eggs	2		
flour	3 cups		
vanilla	1 tsp.		

1. Theo and Krista are baking cookies for the booth. The recipe makes 2 dozen cookies, but they need to bake 6 dozen. How much of each ingredient will they need?

   a) To go from 2 dozen to 6 dozen, _____ each ingredient by 3.

   b) Fill in the chart with your results.

2. The booth was so popular that they need twice as many cookies the next day. Krista and her mom bake 12 dozen more cookies. How much of each ingredient will they need?

   a) To go from 2 dozen to 12 dozen, multiply each ingredient by _____.

   b) Fill in the chart with your results.

Class Survey

After the carnival, Mr. Lim took a class survey. He wanted to see which activities children liked the most. This is what the graph looked like when they were done.

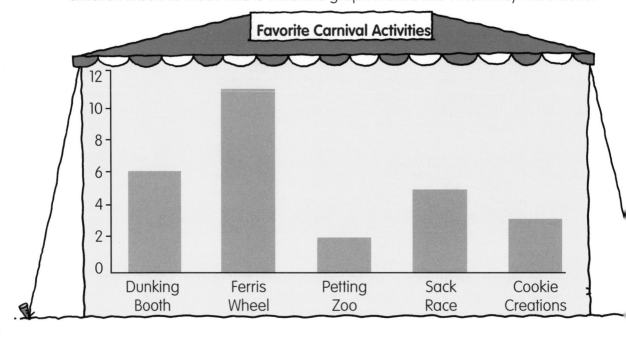

1. How many children liked each activity best?
   Dunking Booth: _____   Ferris Wheel: _____   Petting Zoo: _____
   Sack Race: _____   Cookie Creations: _____

2. How many children are in Mr. Lim's class? _____

3. How many children liked the petting zoo, sack race, and Ferris wheel combined? _____

4. Which activity was the least popular? _____

5. Which two activities added together equal the most popular activity?
   _____ and _____

6. How many more children liked the dunking booth than Cookie Creations?

   _____

Shifty Shapes

Solve the problems. Remember, congruent figures have the same shape and size.

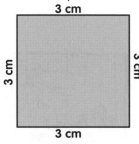

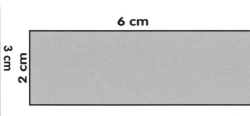

1. Are these shapes congruent?

YES   NO

Explain your answer: _____

_____

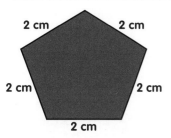

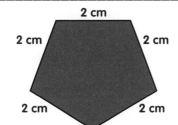

2. Are these shapes congruent?

YES   NO

Explain your answer: _____

_____

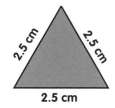

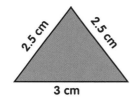

3. Are these shapes congruent?

YES   NO

Explain your answer: _____

_____

4. Draw a congruent shape next to each of these shapes.

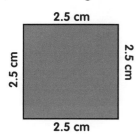

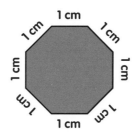

Great Gardens

Perimeter is the total distance around a figure. Kim is planting gardens with her grandpa. What is the perimeter of each garden?

1. The flower garden is shaped like a rectangle.

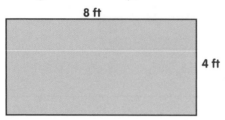

8 ft

4 ft

What is the perimeter of the flower garden? _____

2. The vegetable garden is 12 feet long on two sides.
   The other two sides are half as long.
   What is the perimeter of the vegetable garden? _____

12 ft

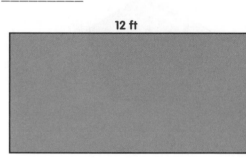

3. Grandpa is also planting an herb garden. This garden will be shaped like a triangle. What is the perimeter of the herb garden?

_____

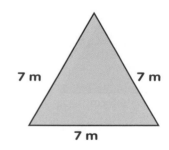

7 m   7 m

7 m

4. The last garden is just for strawberries. It has an odd shape with five sides. What is the perimeter of the strawberry garden? _____

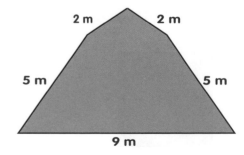

2 m   2 m

5 m   5 m

9 m

Veggies for Sale

1. Luke has $1.00. He bought 2 pounds of celery and 5 pounds of corn. How many pounds of tomatoes can he buy with the money he has left over?

   _____

2. Cherie bought 3 pounds of carrots, 6 pounds of eggplants, and 4 pounds of tomatoes. She has a $5.00 bill. How much change did she get back?

   _____

3. Shana bought two times more celery than carrots. She bought half as many beans as celery. She bought 4 pounds of carrots. How much did Shana spend altogether? _____

4. Jared bought three times more eggplants than beans. He bought four times more tomatoes than eggplants. He bought 2 pounds of beans. If Jared has $5.00, how much change did he get back? _____

What Am I?

Solve each problem. Then draw the shape described.

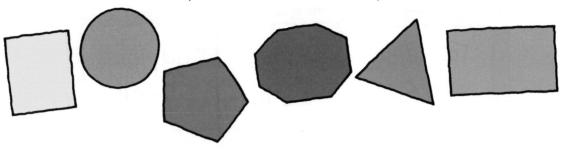

1. I have four sides.
   My top and bottom are the same length.
   My sides are the same length.
   My sides are half the length of my top.
   What am I?

   _____

2. I don't have any corners or angles.
   I don't have any sides.
   I am perfectly round.
   What am I?

   _____

3. I am a polygon.
   I have eight sides.
   All of my sides are the same length.
   What am I?

   _____

Measuring Up

1. Mia's sunflower is 84 inches tall. How many feet tall is it?

   _____ feet

   How many yards and inches tall is it?

   _____ yards and

   _____ inches

2. Marco needs 9 yards of garden hose to reach all the plants in the backyard. He already has 14 feet of hose. How many more feet does he need? _____ feet

3. There are 1.6 kilometers in a mile. Tana walked 3 miles with her friends to the apple orchard. How many kilometers did they walk? _____ kilometers

4. There are 16 ounces in a pound. Derek picked 8 pounds of apples. Leah picked 144 ounces of apples. Whose apples weighed the most? _____

Dinnertime!

Jason, Carly, Serena, and Rashid each ordered their favorite dinners.

The dinners were spaghetti, a hamburger, salad, and tacos.

Use the clues to match each child with his or her dinner.

Rashid's dinner is an Italian dish.

The name of Carly's dinner begins with an "S."

Serena ordered tacos.

	Spaghetti	Hamburger	Salad	Tacos
Jason				
Carly				
Serena				
Rashid				

In Season

Caleb, Juvia, Brian, and Sara each have a favorite season. Can you figure out what season each child likes best? Read the clues to find out.

Brian spends his favorite season skiing in Utah.

Sara's favorite season begins with the same letter as her name.

Caleb likes this season because the snow melts.

	Winter	Summer	Fall	Spring
Caleb				
Juvia				
Brian				
Sara				

Cooking Class

Ms. Gable is having a cooking class for the neighborhood kids.
Before they start cooking, she wants them to practice their measurements.
She gave them a measurements list.

Measurements

8 ounces (oz.) = 1 cup
16 ounces (oz.) = 1 pound
2 cups = 1 pint (pt.)
2 pints = 1 quart (qt.)
4 quarts = 1 gallon
3 teaspoons (tsp.) =
1 tablespoon (Tbs.)

1. Sam has 4 pints of cream. He needs 4 oz. for cream
   sauce and 12 oz. for cheesecake.
   a) How many cups does he need? _____
   b) How many ounces are leftover? _____

2. Eliza has 3 cups of chocolate chips. She needs 8 oz. for cookies
   and $1\frac{1}{4}$ cups for brownies.
   a) How many ounces does she need? _____
   b) How many ounces are leftover? _____

3. Jerome has a recipe that calls for 3 pounds of ground beef and 2 quarts of tomato sauce. He's going to split the recipe in half to make two batches.

    a) How many ounces of ground beef are in each batch? _____

    b) How many cups of tomato sauce are in each batch? _____

4. Jessica forgot her glasses. She added 10 times more Tbs. of butter than was needed. The recipe called for only 2 Tbs.

    a) How many tablespoons of butter did she add? _____

    b) How many teaspoons should she take out? _____

5. Deena needs 2 gallons of apple cider for her cinnamon spice punch. She has 6 only pints.

    a) How many more cups of cider does she need? _____

    b) How many more ounces of cider does she need? _____

6. Clay is making snicker doodle cookies. The recipe, which makes 2 dozen, calls for $\frac{1}{2}$ Tbs. of vanilla. Clay is making 12 dozen cookies.

    a) How many teaspoons of vanilla will he need? _____

    b) How many cookies will he make? _____

Cooking Quiz

Ms. Gable is making some recipes much bigger. They are going to have a feast! Help the children fill in the recipe charts.

Spaghetti Sauce

Ingredient	1 recipe	4 recipes	15 recipes
tomato sauce	4 cups		
chicken stock	$2\frac{1}{2}$ cups		
ground beef	2 pounds		
garlic	6 cloves		
basil	3 Tbs.		
onion	1 cup		

Lemonade

Ingredient	1 recipe	3 recipes	10 recipes
lemons	6		
water	$4\frac{1}{2}$ cups		
sugar	$\frac{1}{2}$ cup		

Guessin[g] [Ga]me

Read the clues to fin[d the correct n]umber.

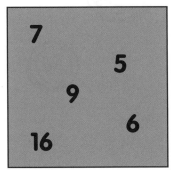

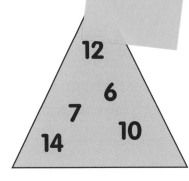

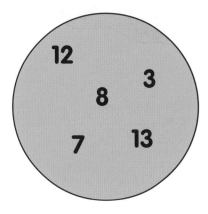

1. It is not an odd number.

    It is in the triangle and the circle.

    It is more than 8.

    What is the number? _____

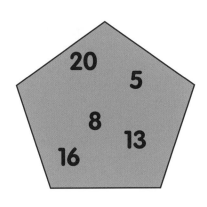

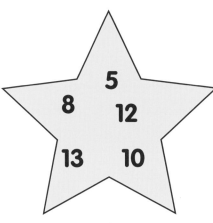

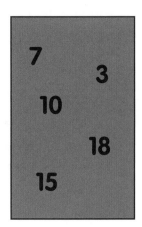

2. It is an even number.

    It is not in the pentagon.

    It is less than 13.

    It is divisible by 5.

    What is the number? _____

Shopping Spree

1. Toni wants to take tennis lessons. Each lesson costs $2.50.
   She wants to take 10 lessons. Her dad gave her $10.00.
   She has saved $6.50. How much more does she need to save?

   _____ 18.50 _____

2. Sean wants new tennis shoes. The shoes cost $18.00.
   He is mowing lawns to save money. He makes $2.35 per lawn.
   How many lawns does Sean need to mow to save enough
   money for the shoes? _____

3. Ana took $25.00 to the mall. First, she bought ice cream for herself
   and her two friends at $1.75 each. Then she bought a dress for
   $12.75. If she wants to buy a video game for $10.99, does she have
   enough money? _____ NO _____

4. Michael is saving for a new bike. He makes $5.25 a week
   at the bookstore. The new bike costs $59.99. He has already
   saved $24.62. How many more weeks will he have to work
   to buy the bike? _____

Time for Sports

Read each problem carefully. Some problems have
information you don't need. Cross out any information
you don't need to solve the problem.

1. Dylan's baseball game started at 12:30 PM. They sang "Take Me Out to the
   Ballgame" during the seventh inning stretch. It lasted 2 hours and 45 minutes.
   What time did the game end? _____

2. Shaniqua played in two tennis matches. The first one lasted from 10:00 AM to
   11:15 AM. She won the match. The second one lasted from 12:15 PM to 1:45 PM.
   How long did she play altogether?

   _____ hours _____ minutes

3. Justin got to the skateboard park at 2:30 PM. He met
   his three friends there. His mom picked him up 3
   hours and 20 minutes later. What time did Justin
   leave the skateboard park?

   _____

4. Dani began her first volleyball game at 1:15 PM. She
   played for 1 hour. Then there was a 15-minute break.
   Her second volleyball game lasted 45 minutes. She
   scored the most points. What time was Dani done
   playing?

   _____

Bianca's Busy Day

Bianca has a busy schedule! Read her schedule below.
Then answer the questions.

7:00 AM	Get up and eat breakfast
7:45 AM	Catch the bus to school
8:15 AM	School begins
11:10 AM	Eat lunch
12:45 PM	Read to kindergarten students
2:20 PM	School gets out
2:30 PM	Mom picks her up for soccer practice
3:45 PM	Soccer practice ends
4:15 PM	Walk neighbor's dogs
4:45 PM	Feed and play with the hamsters
5:00 PM	Homework
6:00 PM	Help with dinner
6:30 PM	Eat dinner
7:30 PM	Favorite TV show
9:15 PM	Bedtime

1. It is _____ hours and _____ minutes between
   breakfast and lunch.

2. How long does soccer practice last? _____

3. How long does Bianca spend with the animals? _____

4. Bianca got up at 6:15 AM one morning to walk the dogs. It took her 20 minutes. Afterward, she spent 30 minutes getting ready for school. Did she catch the bus on time? _____

5. It is _____ hours and _____ minutes between lunch and dinner.

6. Bianca's mom gets out of work at 1:45 PM. She got stuck in traffic. It took her 55 minutes to get to school. Did she pick up Bianca on time?

_____

7. Bianca's school day lasts _____ hours and _____ minutes.

8. Bianca wants to walk the dogs and play with the hamsters between dinner and her favorite TV show. Does she have time? _____

Big on Baseball

Problems need to include enough information for you to solve them.
Read each problem carefully. If there is enough information, solve the problem.
If there isn't, put an X on the line. Then tell what is missing.

1. Shana pitched part of yesterday's baseball game. She threw 14 pitches in the first three innings. Then she threw 17 in each remaining inning. How many pitches did she throw altogether? _____
   What's missing? _____

2. Viet hit two grand slam home runs this season. Four runs are scored for each grand slam. If he hits 3 more grand slams this season, it will be a new league record. If he breaks the record, how many runs will have scored as a result?

   _____
   What's missing? _____

3. There are 9 players on the field for each team. Ten teams are playing in today's tournament. Exactly one third of the players are girls. How many players are girls? _____
   What's missing? _____

4. Gabriel is the best hitter on the Cougars team. He brought in a total of 18 runs the first half of the season. How many hits will he have to bring in by the end of the season to break the league record? _____
   What's missing? _____

   _____

Time Teasers

Time is measured in seconds, minutes, and hours.

60 seconds = 1 minute

60 minutes = 1 hour

24 hours = 1 day

1. The animal shelter opens at 10:00 AM every day
   except Sunday. It's closed on Sunday. It closes at 6:30 PM.
   How many minutes is the shelter open per day? _____
   How many hours is the shelter open per week? _____

2. Gigi starts work 1 hour after the shelter opens. She works $3\frac{1}{2}$ hours.
   What time does she get off work? _____
   How many minutes does Gigi work? _____

3. Michael walks the dogs for 40 minutes each day. Then he feeds and grooms the
   rabbits. That usually takes him 1 hour. On the days that begin with a "T," Michael
   plays with the cats for 30 minutes too.
   How many minutes does Michael work at the shelter on the days that
   begin with "T"? _____

   How many hours does Michael work at the shelter each week? _____

4. The shelter employs 22 volunteers. Each volunteer must put in at least 4 hours
   per week. Half of the volunteers put in 8 hours per week.
   How many hours do all the volunteers work per week?

   _____

Football Fun

Here are some football facts.

Touchdown = 6 Points   Football Field = 100 Yards

Field Goal = 3 Points   Players on Each Team = 11

Safety = 2 Points   First Down = 10 Yards

4 Quarters in a Game

Hint: Every time a team scores a touchdown,
it gets a chance to kick one extra point.

Now figure out these problems about the game of football

1. Team A scored 2 touchdowns in the first quarter and 1 in the third.
   But it missed one of its extra points. Team B scored 4 field goals
   and 1 touchdown in the last quarter. It made its extra point.
   Who won the game? _____
   What was the final score? Team A _____ Team B _____

2. Team A is on its own 25-yard line.
   What percentage of the field has it covered? _____
   What fraction of the field has it covered? _____

3. The kickoff return player caught the ball at the 18-yard line.
   He ran to his own 45-yard line before he was tackled.
   How many yards did he gain? _____

4. Team A is at the 49-yard line. Someone was called for a foul. The team got a 15-yard penalty and must go back 15 yards. Where does the referee spot the ball? _____

5. By the third quarter, Team B had scored 34 points. They didn't score any safeties or field goals.
   How many touchdowns did they score? _____
   Did they make all of their extra points? _____

6. Each game has four 15-minute quarters. There is a 10-minute break between each quarter for commercial breaks.
   How long does the game last in hours? _____
   How long does the game last in minutes? _____

7. Team B is on the 50-yard line. On the next play, the quarterback completes a 25-yard pass.
   After this play, what percentage of the field will they have covered? _____
   What fraction of the field will they have covered? _____

Map It Out

Study the map. Then answer the questions on the next page.

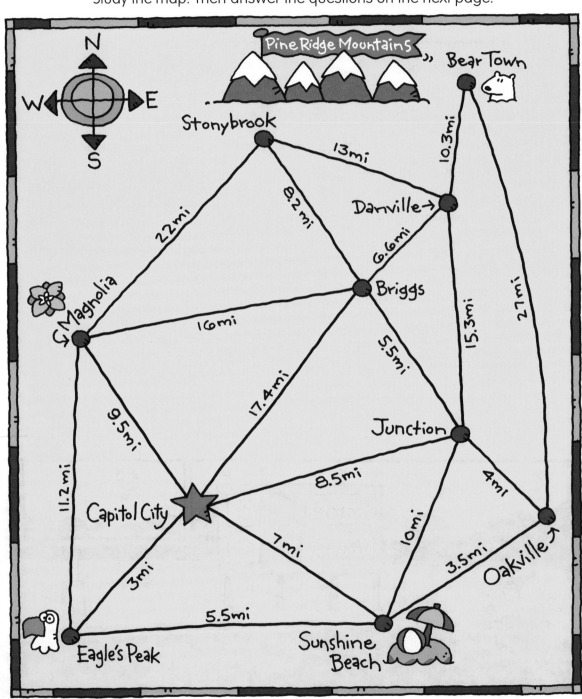

1. Ben took the train from Eagle's Peak to Junction. He went through Capitol City. Then he drove to Danville.
   a) How many miles did he travel altogether? _____
   b) If he went through Sunshine Beach, how many miles would he travel?

   _____

2. Krista wants to find the shortest route from Sunshine Beach to Stonybrook.
   a) How many miles is the shortest route? _____
   b) Through what cities would she travel? _____

   _____

3. The Charles family drove from Capitol City to Magnolia for the state fair. Then they finished their vacation in Bear Town.
   a) How many total miles would they travel if they took the shortest route?

   _____
   b) Through what cities would they travel? _____

4. Emily took the train to see her sister in Oakville. Emily lives in Magnolia. On the way there, she went through Briggs and Junction. On the way back, she went through Sunshine Beach, Capitol City, and Eagle's Peak.
   a) Which way was longer, the way there or the way back? _____
   b) How many miles was the longest route? _____
   c) How many total miles was Emily's roundtrip? _____

All About Area

To find the area, multiply length by width.

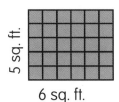

Length = 5 square feet (sq. ft.)

Width = 6 square feet (sq. ft.)

Area = length x width = 5 x 6 = 30 square feet (sq. ft.)

The Gonzales family is building a new house. They need to plan out the square footage of each room. Write a number sentence for each problem.

1.

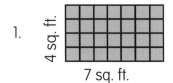

Area of Kitchen = _____

2.

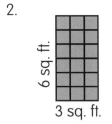

Area of Kristina's Room = _____

3.

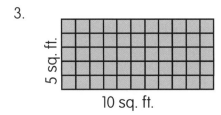

Area of Living Room = _____

4.

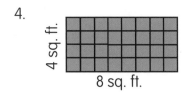

Area of Emilio's Room = _____

Picture Problems

Remember, area = length x width.

Use this formula to figure out the area of each object.

Draw a picture to show the object. Label your drawings.

Write number sentences to show how you got your answers.

1. Terrance bought a map of the United States. It is 9 in. high and 20 in. long.

   What is the area of the map?

   Area = _____

2. Mr. Greer's class is painting two murals for charity. One is 25 ft. x 6 ft.

   The other is 14 ft. x 8 ft. What is the area of both murals put together?

   Area = _____

3. Nicole needs hay to cover the floors of her horse stalls. Each stall is 12 ft. x 10 ft.

   There are 8 stalls. What is the area Nicole needs to cover?

   Area = _____

Plot the Graph

Kerri opened a gourmet chocolate shop in May. She wrote down the number of sales she made each month. But to compare sales for the year, she needs to plot them on a graph. Plot the information on Kerri's list on the graph below.

1. Begin by finding the month of May at the bottom of the graph. This is when she opened the store.

2. Then go up 350 and plot the point. These are the sales for May.

3. After plotting the points for all months, go back and connect the points with a line. This allows you to compare sales over the year.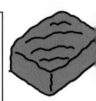

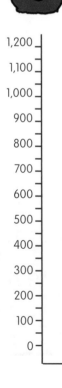

May **350**	June **125**	July **425**	Aug. **550**
Sept. **675**	Oct. **400**	Nov. **750**	Dec. **1,100**
Jan. **850**	Feb. **925**	Mar. **700**	Apr. **850**

```
1,200 _
1,100 _
1,000 _
  900 _
  800 _
  700 _
  600 _
  500 _
  400 _
  300 _
  200 _
  100 _
    0 _
        May   June   July   Aug.   Sept.   Oct.   Nov.   Dec.   Jan.   Feb.   Mar.   Apr.
```

Now read the graph to answer these questions.

1. In which month did sales peak?

_____

2. How many more sales did Kerri make in December than in November?

_____

3. Which two months had the same number of sales?

_____

4. In which month were sales the lowest?

_____

5. What is the difference in sales between the highest and lowest month?

_____

6. Look at the overall graph. Do you think Kerri's Gourmet Chocolates will succeed as a business? Why or why not?

_____

_____

Weighing In

Read each problem carefully.

Then solve the problem. Show your work.

1. Maya shipped three boxes home from Italy. They weighed 26.5 pounds, 15.2 pounds, and 19.8 pounds. It cost 10¢ per pound to ship the packages. How much did she spend? _____

2. Derek carried all the suitcases into the airport. They weighed 35.7 pounds, 22.5 pounds, 17 pounds, and 48.4 pounds. What is the average weight he carried? _____ pounds

3. Sara's shopping cart was filled with vegetables. She had 14.6 ounces of asparagus, 9.5 ounces of green beans, 15.3 ounces of celery, and 10.4 ounces of garlic. If she is going to divide up the vegetables evenly between 5 people in her family, how many ounces will each person get? (Hint: Round up.) _____ ounces

4. Emily weighed each cat at the shelter. One cat weighed 8.6 pounds, one weighed 12.5 pounds, and one weighed 15.8 pounds. What is the average weight of the cats? _____ pounds

Piece of the Pie

Write a number sentence for each picture.

Then solve the problem.

Change fractions to mixed numbers, if needed.

Hint: Write fractions to represent the shaded part of each pie.

1.

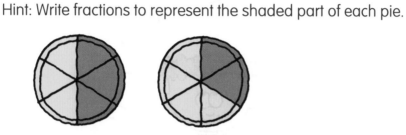

——————— + ——————— = ———————

2.

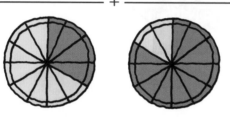

——————— + ——————— = ———————

3.

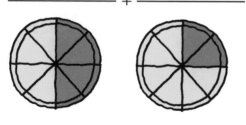

——————— + ——————— = ———————

4.

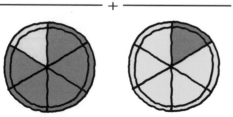

——————— + ——————— = ———————

Perfect Patterns

Can you guess the patterns? Write the rule for each pattern.
Then fill in the missing number.

1.

25	5
55	11
10	
100	20
35	7

Rule: _____

2.

10	17
3	10
9	16
12	
26	33

Rule: _____

3.

4	32
6	
10	80
12	96
8	64

Rule: _____

4.

72	60
24	12
15	
12	0
36	24

Rule: _____

Step by Step

Carefully read each problem. Then decide which steps you
should take to solve it. Write the steps in order.

1. Chelsea ate $\frac{3}{12}$ of the pizza for lunch. She ate $\frac{6}{12}$ of the pizza for
   dinner. How much pizza does she have left?
   Step 1: _____
   Step 2: _____
   Answer: _____

2. Ahmed collects racecars. He has 24 total. He's giving half of his
   cars to his 2 brothers. They each get the same number of cars.
   How many cars does each brother get?
   Step 1: _____
   Step 2: _____
   Answer: _____

3. Rea scored 5 runs in the season's first softball game. She
   scored 6 runs in the second game, and 4 in the third. How
   many runs did she average for all three games?
   Step 1: _____
   Step 2: _____
   Answer: _____

Age Challenge

Compare the age of each person.
Then answer the questions.

Brooke is 30 years older than Trey. Chase is 16 years older than Brooke.
Lisa is 8 years younger than Trey. Trey is 12 years old.

1. Write the people's names in order, from youngest to oldest.

_____

_____

_____

_____

2. What age is Lisa? _____

3. What age is Chase? _____

4. How many years older than Lisa is Brooke?_____

5. How many years younger than Chase is Trey? _____

On the Road

Read the problem and compare the distances.

Then answer the questions.

Sarah lives in Sunset Beach. Shasta is 103.6 miles away. Cherryvale is 55.7 miles further than Shasta. Barrington is 27.3 miles closer than Cherryvale. Pebble Beach is 38.4 miles farther than Cherryvale. Penning is 64.5 miles away from Sunset Beach.

1. Write the city names in order, from closest to furthest to Sunset Beach.
   Write the mileage next to each city.

   _____

   _____

   _____

   _____

   _____

2. How many miles is it from Sunset Beach to Shasta?

   _____

3. How many miles is it from Barrington to Cherryvale?

   _____

4. How many miles is it from Penning to Shasta if Penning is on the route from
   Sunset Beach to Shasta?

   _____

Picnic Feast

There were 4,638 ants at the Merrick family picnic. What a feast! Find out what happened next. Then solve the problems.

1. 325 ants went for the watermelon. 730 ants went for the fried chicken. But a whopping 1,210 went for the potato chips!

   a) How many more ants went for the potato chips than the watermelon? _____

   b) How many ants did not go after any of these foods? _____

2. Twice as many ants dove into the ice cream as went for the fried chicken. Half as many ants that went for the potato chips took a swim in the lemonade.

   a) How many ants dove into the ice cream? _____

   b) How many ants took a swim in the lemonade? _____

3. 2,155 ants didn't like what they found at the Merrick picnic. They moved on to the Barkley picnic. 1,492 ants then moved from the Barkley picnic to the Simon picnic.

   a) How many ants were left at the Merrick picnic? _____

   b) How many ants were left at the Barkley picnic? _____

Cupcake Corner

Circle the cupcakes to represent each fraction.
Then solve the problem.

1.

$$\frac{4}{8} \quad + \quad \frac{3}{8} = \underline{\hspace{2cm}}$$

2.

$$\frac{9}{12} \quad + \quad \frac{6}{12} = \underline{\hspace{2cm}}$$

3.

$$\frac{5}{10} \quad + \quad \frac{2}{5} = \underline{\hspace{2cm}}$$

4.

$$\frac{1}{3} \quad + \quad \frac{5}{6} = \underline{\hspace{2cm}}$$

Is It Congruent?

Congruent figures are the exact same shape and size. Circle YES if the shapes are congruent. Circle NO if they're not congruent.

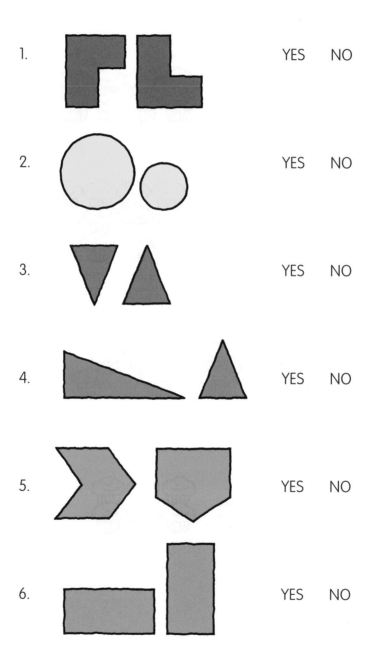

1. YES   NO

2. YES   NO

3. YES   NO

4. YES   NO

5. YES   NO

6. YES   NO

Pet Combinations

Joey adopted 3 kittens (calico, striped, and orange)
and 2 puppies (beagle and chow). How many different combinations
of kittens and puppies can he make? Hint: Joey is making combos in pairs.

Begin by writing the kittens across the top of the chart
and the puppies down the side.

	calico	_____	_____
beagle			
_____			

Joey can make _____ combinations.

What's the Rule?

Can you guess the patterns? Write the rule for each pattern.
Then fill in the missing numbers.

1.

96	8
132	11
48	
24	2
	7

Rule: _____

2.

3	9
10	100
	25
4	16
8	

Rule: _____

3.

13	3
25	15
80	70
	0
62	

Rule: _____

4.

16	25
	30
44	53
12	21
57	

Rule: _____

First Day of School

Emma can't decide which outfit to wear on the first day of school. She has loafers, sandals, sneakers, and boots. She also has jeans, a dress, khakis, and a skirt.

What clothing combinations can she wear?

Begin by writing the shoes across the top of the chart and the clothes down the side.

	_____	_____	_____	_____
_____				
_____				
_____				
_____				

Emma can make _____ combinations.

Unusual Pets

Use the information in the chart to answer the questions.

Name	rat	snake	ferret	pot-bellied pig
Katie	3	1	0	1
David	1	0	4	2
Enzo	5	3	1	0
Jenna	0	3	3	1
Kevin	7	0	2	4

1. Who doesn't have any snakes? __David__ and __Kevin__

2. Who has the same number of snakes and ferrets? __Jenna__

3. Who owns the least number of unusual pets? __Katie__

4. How many more rats does Kevin have than David? __0__

5. How many more ferrets than snakes do the children have? __3__

6. How many unusual pets do the children have altogether? __41__

Various Variables

Variables can help you solve problems.
Use variables to make equations and find the mystery numbers.

Example: Kyle washed 6 dogs on Saturday and a mystery number on Monday. He washed 15 dogs in all. How many dogs did he wash on Monday?   Equation: $6 + n = 15$

Answer: $6 + 9 = 15$

Make an equation for each problem. Use a variable to represent the mystery number. Then solve the problem.

1. Shelby put 46 apples in the basket. A mystery number rolled out. When Shelby got back, there were only 27 apples left in the basket. How many apples rolled out?
   Equation: _____ $46 - \_ = 27$ _____
   Answer: _____ 19 _____

2. Carlos bought 6 t-shirts for school. Each shirt cost $12. What mystery number did he spend on all the t-shirts?
   Equation: _____
   Answer: _____

3. Maile ran 3 miles each day for a mystery number of days. At the end of this time, she had run 42 miles. How many days did she run?
   Equation: _____
   Answer: _____

Making Equations

Use a variable to write an equation for each problem. Then solve the problem.

1. The Tigers scored a mystery number of points in the first three games of the season. They scored 307 points in the next three games. They scored a total of 648 points for all six games. How many points did they score in the first three games?

   Equation: _____

   Answer: _____

2. Nick collected 275 baseball cards. He stores an equal number of cards in 5 different boxes. What is the mystery number of baseball cards stored in each box?

   Equation: _____

   Answer: _____

3. Kayla bought a bag of chocolate candies. The whole bag cost $1.00. The bag holds 20 candies. What is the mystery cost of each individual candy?

   Equation: _____

   Answer: _____

4. Charles counted 473 stars in the sky on Tuesday. On Wednesday, he counted only 188. What mystery number of stars more did he count on Tuesday than Wednesday?

   Equation: _____

   Answer: _____

Magic Number

28

Read the clues. Cross out the numbers in the balloons
to find the magic number.

56

1. It's not 12 + 16.

2. It's not 72 ÷ 9.

30

3. It's not 42 − 12.

45

4. It's not 3 x 11.

5. It's not 5 x 4.

6. It's not 53 − 8.

20

7. It's not 16 x 4.

8

8. It's not 25 + 18.

9. It's not 108 ÷ 9.

10. It's not 7 x 7.

12

64

43

49

33

The magic number is _____.

Extra Information

Read each problem carefully. Some problems have
information you don't need. Cross out any information you
don't need to solve the problem. Then solve it.

1. Darla has a piece of canvas with an area of 45 square feet. She's going to paint a
   mural for her school. She will mount the mural on a wall that is 12 ft. x 4 ft.

   a) Will the canvas cover the entire wall? _____
   b) If not, how many square feet are leftover? _____

2. Sean has 14 pounds of soil for the garden. It will cover an area of 60 square feet.
   The garden is actually 30 ft. x 3 ft.
   a) What is the area of the garden? _____
   b) How many more pounds of soil will Sean need? _____

3. Jeff's class is studying a frog's life cycle. He has 40 frogs to pass out to his
   classmates. The class is divided into 8 groups.
   a) How many frogs does each group get? _____
   b) If the class is divided into 10 groups, how many frogs does each group get?

   _____

4. Shana gave $\frac{3}{10}$ of her cookies to her brother. She gave another $\frac{1}{10}$ to her friend.
   She ate another $\frac{3}{10}$ herself.
   a) How many cookies did Shana give away?

   _____

   b) How many cookies does Shana have left?

   _____

Around the Table

For lunch, the Booker children eat their favorite pizzas. Which kind of pizza is each child's favorite? Read the clues to find out. Then write each child's name and favorite pizza on the lines around the table. The first clue has been filled in for you.

The children are:

Joy

Connor

Blake

Alicia

The pizza types are:

pepperoni

cheese

pineapple

mushroom

Clues:

1. Alicia does not sit next to the brother who eats cheese.

2. The sister who eats pineapple sits to Alicia's left.

3. Connor does not eat cheese or mushrooms.

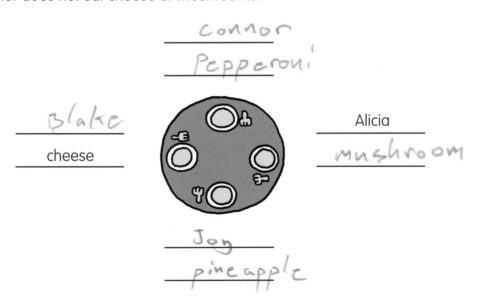

Connor
Pepperoni

Blake

cheese

Alicia

mushroom

Joy

pineapple

What's Missing?

Problems need to include enough information for you to solve them. Read each problem carefully. If there is enough information, solve the problem. If there isn't, put an X on the line. Then tell what is missing.

1. Zoe kicked 6 goals in the league's first three soccer games. Tran kicked twice as many goals as Blain. Blain kicked 5 more goals than Zoe. How many goals did Tran kick? __22__
   What's missing? _____
   _____

2. Kenny drove his new sports car all around town. He drove 10.5 miles to his friend's house, 15.6 miles to the park, and then 25 miles along the coast. How many gallons of gas did he use? _____
   What's missing? _____

3. There are 60 points on the basketball scoreboard at half time. During the second half, Brianna scored 25% of the points. How many points did she score? _____
   What's missing? _____

4. Wyatt ran in the 100-meter race. He ran it in 8.6 minutes. Kim ran it in 1.4 minutes longer than Wyatt. Jon ran it in half of Kim's time. How long did it take Jon to run the race? _____
   What's missing? _____

Subway Stops

The subway can take you all around town.
Read about the subway and then answer the questions.

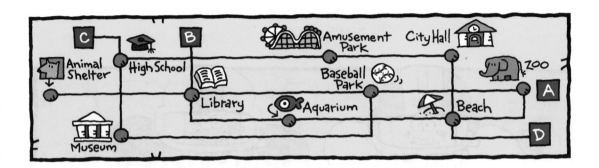

The A train stops at the zoo, the baseball park, the library, and the animal shelter. The B train stops at the library, the aquarium, the beach, and the zoo. The C train stops at the high school, the museum, and the baseball park. The D train stops the beach, city hall, the amusement park, and the high school.

1. How many places could you go on the B and D trains combined? _____8_____

2. Which two trains stop at the high school? ___C D_____

3. Which train stops at both the baseball park and the animal shelter? _____A_____

4. You want to transfer from train A to train B. At what place would

   you transfer? _____

5. Which trains take you to places to visit animals? __A B_____

Football Craze

Read about the football stadium. Then solve the problems.

The Blizzards are playing the Hurricanes today. The football stadium has 5,375 regular seats and 250 VIP seats.

1. 3,997 tickets were sold by Thursday. Another 1,280 were sold on Friday. How many tickets are left? _____

2. In the regular seats, Section A holds 1,200 people, Section B holds 1,250 people, and Section C holds 1,365 people. If there are only 4 sections, how many people does Section D hold? _____

3. Look at how many tickets were left in question 1. On Saturday, 127 Section A tickets were sold, 104 Section B tickets were sold, and 73 VIP tickets were sold. Did the game sell out? _____

4. The Jameson family bought 2 VIP tickets for $50 each. Then they bought 6 Section C tickets for $26.00 each. How much money did they spend? _____

School Daze

Read each problem carefully and then solve it. Show your work.

1. Tara bought a box of pencils for $1.15, a notebook for $2.25, and a highlighter for $1.99. How much money did Tara spend?
   Name the operation you will use to solve the problem: _____
   Answer: _____

2. Jason is reading a book about giant reptiles. He reads 14 pages per hour. He's been reading for $2\frac{1}{2}$ hours. How many pages has he read?
   Name the operation you will use to solve the problem: _____
   Answer: _____

3. Mrs. Beale has to grade 72 papers over the weekend. She can grade 8 papers per hour. How many hours will it take her to grade all the papers?
   Name the operation you will use to solve the problem: _____
   Answer: _____

4. Daniel helps in the school cafeteria to make extra money. He makes $4.50 per hour. If he worked 4 hours last week, how much money did he make?
   Name the operation you will use to solve the problem: _____
   Answer: _____

Mystery Number

Read the clues. Cross out the numbers in the leaves to find the mystery number.

59

72

1. It's not 12 x 6.

2. It's not 9 x 9.

3. It's not 70 – 7.

45

4. It's not 3 x 15.

5. It's not 100 ÷ 2.

75

6. It's not 7 x 11.

7. It's not 25 x 3.

77

63

8. It's not 8 x 6.

9. It's not 55 + 9.

10. It's not 49 + 10.

64

81

50

68

48

The mystery number is _____.

Reading Circle

Kristin and her friends are all reading different kinds of books.
Read the clues to find out who is reading each book. Write the names
and books on the lines around the reading circle.

The friends' names are:

    Kristin

    Alice

    Ana

    Jose

The books are:

    fairy tale

    biography

    legend

    poetry

Clues:

1. A girl whose name begins with "A" reads poetry. She is sitting to Kristin's right.

2. Kristin is not sitting next to the boy who is reading a legend.

3. Ana does not read poetry or fairy tales.

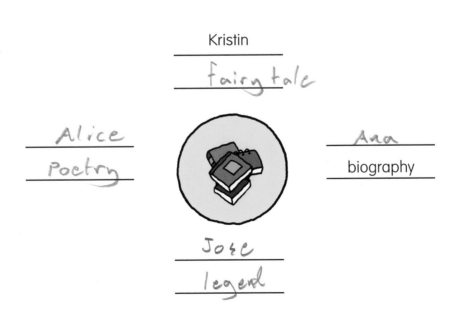

Kristin

fairy tale

Alice
Poetry

Ana
biography

Jose
legend

Movie Mania

You are taking a survey. You want to find out which kinds of movies students like best. Fill in the graph using the information below. (Draw a bar up to the correct number to show your results.) Then answer the questions on the next page.

Ten students like drama the best.

Seven people like animation best.

Half as many students that like drama like scary movies best.

Seven people like comedy best.

If you add together the number of students who like animation and comedy, you'll find out how many like action best.

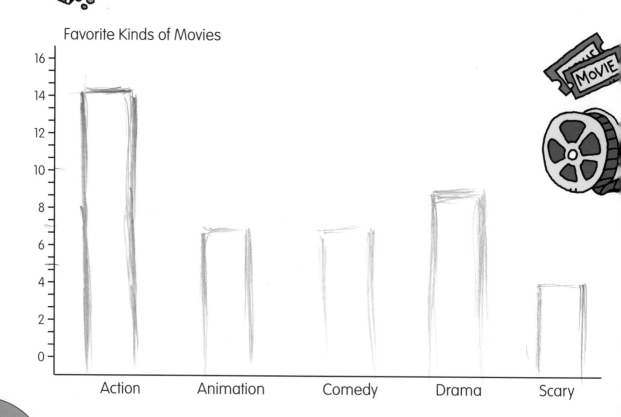

Favorite Kinds of Movies

1. How many students liked each type of movie best?

Action: __14__   Comedy: __7__   Scary: __3__

Animation: __7__   Drama: __0__

2. How many students liked comedy and scary movies together? _____

3. Which two types of movies were liked by the same number of students?

_____

4. How many fewer students liked comedy than drama? _____

5. How many more students liked action movies than animated movies? _____

6. How many students were surveyed altogether? _____

Answer Key

Page 4
1. subtraction; 22 − 11 = 11
2. multiplication; 5 x 4 = 20
3. division; 64 ÷ 2 = 32
4. multiplication;
   .25 x 8 = 2.00 (or $2.00)

Page 5
1. 24 x 2 = 48
2. 18 = 50 − 32
3. 15 + 25 = 40
4. 56 = 7 x 8 or 56 ÷ 7 = 8
5. 85 − 62 = 23 or 85 = 62 + 23
6. 9 x 8 = 72

Page 6
1. (4 x 6) − 9 = 15
2. (55 ÷ 11) x 5 = 25
3. 38 = (6 x 6) + 2
4. 28 + (4 x 7) = 56
5. (8 x 7) − 43 = 13
6. 72 = (81 ÷ 9) x 8

Page 7
1. Step 1: Find out how many marbles Hector has:
   10 x 6 = 60
   Step 2: Divide the number of marbles by the number of friends: 60 ÷ 3 = 20
   Answer: Each friend gets 20 marbles.
2. Step 1: Find out how much popcorn was left after Jenni ate: $\frac{3}{10}$; $\frac{9}{10} - \frac{3}{10} = \frac{6}{10}$
   Step 2: Subtract the amount of popcorn Jenni's sister ate:
   $\frac{6}{10} - \frac{2}{10} = \frac{4}{10}$
   Answer: There was $\frac{4}{10}$ bag of popcorn left.
3. Step 1: Find out how many baseball cards Brett has after selling 8: 32 − 8 = 24
   Step 2: Add the number of cards he bought: 24 + 12 = 36
   Answer: Brett has 36 baseball cards.

Page 8
pepperoni and mushrooms
pepperoni and ham
pepperoni and olives
pepperoni and peppers
mushrooms and ham
mushrooms and olives
mushrooms and peppers
ham and olives
ham and peppers
olive and peppers

Page 9
1a) multiply
2a) 6

Ingredient	2 dozen 1b)	6 dozen	12 dozen 2b)
shortening	1 cup	3 cups	6 cups
sugar	1$\frac{1}{2}$ cups	4$\frac{1}{2}$ cups	9 cups
eggs	2	6	12
flour	3 cups	9 cups	18 cups
vanilla	1 tsps.	3 tsps.	6 tsp.

Page 10
1. Dunking Booth: 6
   Ferris Wheel: 11
   Petting Zoo: 2
   Sack Race: 5
   Cookie Creations: 3
2. 27
3. 18
4. petting zoo
5. Dunking booth, sack race
6. 3

Page 11
1. No; the square has equal sides, and the rectangle has different length sides.
2. Yes; both shapes have an equal number of sides of equal length.
3. No; the triangles are different sizes.
4.

Page 12
1. 24 feet
2. 36 feet
3. 21 meters
4. 23 meters

Page 13
1. 2
2. $2.65
3. $2.68
4. 86¢

Page 14
1. rectangle

2. circle
3. octagon

Page 15
1. 7 feet; 2 yards, 12 inches
2. 13 feet
3. 4.8
4. Leah's

Page 16
Jason: hamburger
Carly: salad
Serena: tacos
Rashid: spaghetti

Page 17
Caleb: spring
Juvia: fall
Brian: winter
Sara: summer

Pages 18–19
1. a) 2 cups, b) 48 ounces
2. a) 18 ounces, b) 6 ounces
3. a) 24 ounces, b) 4 cups
4. a) 20 Tbs., b) 54 tsp.
5. a) 20 cups, b) 160 ounces
6. a) 9 tsp., b) 144 cookies

Page 20
Spaghetti Sauce

Ingredient	1 recipe	4 recipes	15 recipes
tomato sauce	4 cups	16 cups	60 cups
chicken stock	2$\frac{1}{2}$ cups	10 cups	37$\frac{1}{2}$ cups
ground beef	2 pounds	8 pounds	30 pounds
garlic	6 cloves	24 cloves	90 cloves
basil	3 Tbs.	12 Tbs.	45 Tbs.
onion	1 cup	4 cups	15 cups

Lemonade

Ingredient	1 recipe	3 recipes	10 recipes
lemons	6	18	60
water	4$\frac{1}{2}$ cups	13$\frac{1}{2}$ cups	45 cups
sugar	$\frac{1}{2}$ cup	1$\frac{1}{2}$ cup	5 cups

Page 21
1. 12
2. 10

Page 22
1. $8.50
2. 8
3. no
4. 7

Page 23
1. ~~They sang "Take Me Out to the Ballgame" during the seventh inning stretch.~~ 3:15 PM
2. ~~She won the match.~~ 2 hours, 45 minutes
3. ~~He met three friends there.~~ 5:50 PM
4. ~~She scored the most points.~~ 3:15 PM

Pages 24–25
1. 4 hours, 10 minutes
2. 1 hour, 15 minutes
3. 45 minutes
4. yes
5. 7 hours, 20 minutes
6. no
7. 6 hours, 5 minutes
8. yes

Page 26
1. X; need to know how many innings she pitched
2. 20 runs
3. 30 players
4. X; need to know the league record

Page 27
1. 510 minutes; 51 hours
2. 2:30 PM; 210 minutes
3. 130 minutes; 11 hours
4. 132 hours

Pages 28–29
1. Team A; Team A: 20, Team B: 19
2. 25%; $\frac{1}{4}$
3. 27 yards
4. 34 yard line
5. 5; no
6. 1$\frac{1}{2}$ hours; 90 minutes
7. 75%; $\frac{3}{4}$

Pages 30–31
1. a) 26.8 miles, b) 30.8 miles
2. a) 21.2 miles, b) Oakville, Junction, and Briggs
3. a) 42.4 miles, b) Briggs and Danville
4. a) the way there, b) 25.5 miles, c) 50.2 miles

Page 32
1. 7 x 4 = 28 sq. ft.
2. 3 x 6 = 18 sq. ft.
3. 10 x 5 = 50 sq. ft.
4. 8 x 4 = 32 sq. ft.

Page 33
1. 9 x 20 = 180 sq. in.
2. 25 x 6 = 150 sq. ft.; 14 x 8 = 112 sq. ft.; 150 + 112 = 262 sq. ft.
3. 12 x 10 = 120 sq. ft.; 8 x 120 = 960 sq. ft.

Answer Key

Pages 34–35

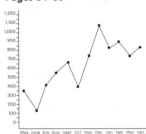

1. December
2. 350
3. January and April
4. June
5. 975
6. Yes; except for October, Kerri's sales seem to be growing through the year.

Page 36
1. $6.15
2. 30.9 pounds
3. 10 ounces
4. 12.3 pounds

Page 37
1. $\frac{3}{6} + \frac{2}{6} = \frac{5}{6}$
2. $\frac{4}{12} + \frac{10}{12} = \frac{14}{12}$ or $1\frac{2}{12}$
3. $\frac{4}{8} + \frac{2}{8} = \frac{6}{8}$
4. $\frac{5}{6} + \frac{1}{6} = \frac{6}{6}$ or 1

Page 38
1. ÷ 5; 2
2. + 7; 19
3. × 8; 48
4. – 12; 3

Page 39
1. Step 1: Find out how much Chelsea ate: $\frac{3}{12} + \frac{6}{12} = \frac{9}{12}$
   Step 2: Subtract the fraction she ate from the whole pizza: $\frac{12}{12} - \frac{9}{12} = \frac{3}{12}$
   Answer: She has $\frac{3}{12}$ of the pizza left.
2. Step 1: Find out how many racecars Ahmed is giving away: 24 ÷ 2 = 12
   Step 2: Divide this number by the 2 brothers: 12 ÷ 2 = 6
   Answer: Each brother gets 6 racecars.
3. Step 1: Find the total runs Rea scored in the first three games: 5 + 6 + 4 = 15

Step 2: Divide this number by the number of games (3):
15 ÷ 3 = 5
Answer: She averaged 5 runs.

Page 40
1. Lisa, Trey, Brooke, Chase
2. 4 years old
3. 58 years old
4. 38 years
5. 46 years

Page 41
1. Penning 64.5; Shasta 103.6; Barrington 132; Cherryvale 159.3; Pebble Beach 197.7
2. 103.6 miles
3. 27.3 miles
4. 39.1 miles

Page 42
1. a) 885, b) 2,373
2. a) 1,460, b) 605
3. a) 2,483, b) 663

Page 43
1. $\frac{7}{8}$
2. $\frac{15}{12}$ or $1\frac{3}{12}$
3. $\frac{9}{10}$
4. $\frac{7}{6}$ or $1\frac{1}{6}$

Page 44
1. yes
2. no
3. yes
4. no
5. no
6. yes

Page 45

	calico	striped	orange
beagle	calico and beagle	striped and beagle	orange and beagle
chow	calico and chow	striped and chow	orange and chow

Joey can make 6 combinations.

Page 46
1. Rule: ÷ 12; 4; 84
2. Rule: number times itself; 5; 64
3. Rule: – 10; 10; 52
4. Rule: + 9; 21; 66

Page 47

	sandals	loafers	sneakers	boots
jeans	jeans/sandals	jeans/loafers	jeans/sneakers	jeans/boots
dress	dress/sandals	dress/loafers	dress/sneakers	dress/boots
khakis	khakis/sandals	khakis/loafers	khakis/sneakers	khakis/boots
skirt	skirt/sandals	skirt/loafers	skirt/sneakers	skirt/boots

Emma can make 16 combinations.

Page 48
1. David and Kevin
2. Jenna
3. Katie
4. 6
5. 3
6. 41

Page 49
1. 46 – n = 27; 19 apples
2. 6 × $12 = n; $72
3. 3 × n = 42; 14 days

Page 50
1. 307 + n = 648; 341 points
2. 275 ÷ 5 = n; 55 cards
3. $1.00 ÷ 20 = n; 5¢
4. 473 – 188 = n; 285 stars

Page 51
The magic number is 56.

Page 52
1. ~~She's going to paint a mural for her school~~; a) no; b) 3 sq. ft.
2. a) 90 sq. ft.; b) 7 pounds
3. ~~Jeff's class is studying a frog's life cycle~~; a) 5 frogs; b) 4 frogs
4. a) $\frac{4}{10}$; b) $\frac{3}{10}$

Page 53

Connor
pepperoni

Blake
cheese

Alicia
mushrooms

Joy
pineapple

Page 54
1. 22 goals
2. X; need to know how many miles per gallon the car gets
3. X; need to know how many points were scored in the second half
4. 5 minutes

Page 55
1. 7
2. trains C and D
3. train A
4. library
5. trains A and B

Page 56
1. 348 tickets
2. 1,560 people
3. no
4. $256

Page 57
1. addition; $5.39
2. multiplication; 35 pages
3. division; 9 hours
4. multiplication; $18

Page 58
The mystery number is 68.

Page 59

Kristin
fairy tales

Alice
poetry

Ana
biography

Jose
legend

Page 60

Page 61
1. action: 14, animation: 7, comedy: 7, drama: 10, scary: 5
2. 12 students
3. comedy and animation
4. 3 students
5. 7 students
6. 43 students